The Quantity of a Hazelnut

The Quantity of
a Hazelnut

Fae Malania

Seabury Books
an imprint of Church Publishing, Inc.,
New York, New York

To the happy memory of my dear husband Leo

An earlier edition of these essays was published in 1968
by Alfred A. Knopf, Inc.

A catalog record for this book is available from the
Library of Congress.

ISBN:1-59627-014-4

Printed in the United States of America.

Church Publishing, Incorporated
445 Fifth Avenue
New York, New York 10016

3 1571 00232 0326

FOREWORD

by Lauren F. Winner

THE BOOK YOU ARE holding in your hands is a quiet book, a book that speaks to us in the quiet places of our lives. The touchstones of Fae Malania's spirituality are ordinary, humble things. Indeed, *The Quantity of a Hazelnut* is interesting in part for its place in literary and pop culture history. Today, a genre of spiritual writing we might call "musings on the everyday" is all the rage. Memoirists from Maya Angelou to Kathleen Norris have come to understand their everyday experiences as the landscape on which the spiritual life unfolds, and the title of one of Norris's books makes this point nicely: *The Quotidian Mysteries: Liturgy, Laundry, and Women's Work.* Not only memoirists, but many, many others increasingly attend not only to the Christian life that takes place in church, or when we go on a spiritual retreat, or when we carve thirty precious minutes from our day to pray. We are beginning to rediscover that the Christian life also unfolds in ordinary time: when we do the dishes, when we garden, when we tuck our children into bed, even when we argue with our spouses. Fae Malania recognized this truth half a century ago. In these pages, you'll read about her kitchen epiphanies, and the spiritual insights that come to her while reading the newspaper. Fae Malania predicted a trend. She anticipated a turn in how Americans would live out their spirituality.

The title of this book is very apt—it is drawn from one of the visions, or "shewings," of the fourteenth-century mystic, Dame Julian of Norwich. In her vision Julian sees something very small, about the size of a hazelnut, lying in the palm of her hand. "What can this be?" she asks. "It is all that is made," is the answer. Julian worries: because it is so small, might not the hazelnut—a synecdoche of all creation—disappear, or be obliterated? Again comes the reassuring answer: "It lasts and ever shall last because God loves it."

Fae Malania's book, which opens with Julian's vision, can be seen as an extended meditation, or riff, on the small hazelnut lying in her hand. The spirituality you will encounter in this book is, like Julian's, profoundly creational. God loves and delights in creation. Indeed, both Julian and Malania recognize that creation "lasts and ever shall, *because* God loves it"—that our very lives are sustained by the ground of God's love. Something as seemingly insignificant as a hazelnut can stand in for all of creation, and, like the hazelnut, all of creation is cradled in God's hand.

I have read *The Quantity of a Hazelnut* several times. Most recently, I read it during Lent. I was struck by Fae Malania's refusal to brook fools. Yes, her spirituality is robustly creational—but it is never namby-pamby. She is well aware of the power of sin. Her book is made grave, at times, by her painful awareness of the myriad ways the world is fractured and yet she remains steadfast in her faith that sin is vanquished by Christ's blood. In this way, too, Malania's spirituality hearkens back to Julian. For is not the quantity of a hazelnut, in Julian's or Fae Malania's hands, like the head of a nail in the palm of Christ?

Fae Malania's lovely book is a small offering, like a hazelnut. Like the hazelnut, it is a reminder of God's love. And like a hazelnut, it can unlock a world.

ABOUT THE AUTHOR

by Marly Youmans

"JUST LITTLE REFLECTIONS that came into my head and I wrote them down in a lined notebook, and eventually I saw that they might add up to something": the reflections that make up Fae Malania's *The Quantity of a Hazelnut* began in this simple, modest manner. Born Faye Etheldra East in 1919, she was educated in her beloved California and at the National Cathedral School in Washington, D. C., where she was confirmed as an Episcopalian, and graduated from Swarthmore College in 1940. Afterward she came to New York for a series of uninteresting clerical jobs—"in those days women didn't expect anything else"—and then worked as assistant to the managing editor of *Mademoiselle* for almost ten years, a job she enjoyed and that led her to write on a regular basis.

In 1950 she married Russian-born Leo Malania, a member of Canada's Department of External Affairs. At the founding of the United Nations, he had accompanied the Canadian delegation to New York, where he was asked to serve under the principal aide to the Secretary-General.

Marriage brought enormous changes to Fae, for Leo had a young autistic son by a prior marriage; his first wife had committed suicide, and Fae felt that she should be a second mother to the child. In 1951, when Dimitri was six, he came to live with the new couple, and Fae quit her job to become a full-time parent. While he had difficulties with communication and showed compulsive, repetitive behaviors, Fae pays tribute to him as a boy of "amazing goodness of character. He was difficult, but there wasn't a mean bone in his body." It is a measure of Fae's strength and honesty that she says, "I was never sorry, although it was never easy, either."

During this time, Fae began to compose essays. Her husband was her first audience: "Leo always said that I was more alive when I was writing, and I think that was true." She never had the urge to write a novel or stories; she conceived of her essays as a "reflection of the day." They were not, however, connected in the manner of, say, an ongoing journal. Looking back, she claims to have had no set "routine," though she usually finished and typed up the day's work by four o'clock. Her habit was to leave the pages on the table for Leo to read, and soon he "looked forward to finding them on the table when he came home." As soon as a piece was complete, she began thinking about the next one; often some minor spark in an essay became the start of the next. In that sense they were connected. Fae kept on writing. The essays offered here were first gathered into a collection and published by Alfred A. Knopf in 1968.

The arrival of "Dimi" also coincided with a shift in Fae's thinking. She had never been a churchgoer and Leo, raised in the Russian Orthodox Church, was staunchly anti-clerical—still, "I said that we should go to church, and Leo said, *'Certainly not!'* Finally he said, rather crossly, 'We'll go to church if it means that much to you, but we have to go every Sunday.'" Time passed, and little by little the family became part of the church. It's strange how the thing we resist the most can take great, passionate hold; one day Leo asked, "How would you feel if I studied for the Episcopal priesthood?" Fae replied, "Oh, I wondered when you would get to that point."

Before long, Fae the writer was married to Leo Malania the Episcopal priest. He was ordained at the Cathedral of the Incarnation in 1964 and they moved to a church in Cambria Heights, Queens. When they arrived in 1965, much of the congregation of St. David's was white and elderly; under his leadership the church was transformed, becoming a young and largely African American congregation. During these years, Dimi grew up and left home. Throughout the 1960s and 1970s Leo was Coordinator for Revision of the Episcopal

Church's *Book of Common Prayer,* which was first approved in 1976 and then published in 1979.

Fae's mother died in 1984, Leo in 1987, and Dimi in 1990 on the day before his forty-first birthday: a trinity of losses, each set three years apart. Leo died of heart failure; Fae recalls that after his last check-up, "I looked at the doctor, and he looked back with a face that told me." She now lives at the Thanksgiving Home in Cooperstown, New York; her outings are usually to Christ Church, where a recent Quiet Day centered on readings from her essays honored her life and writing. She is part of a long tradition of writers at Christ Church, Cooperstown, the historic village church that has nurtured an abundance of local historians, poets, and fiction writers, including novelist James Fenimore Cooper and nature writer Susan Cooper.

She has gifts that console, and she has won the right to be known and remembered as a maker of graceful, potent essays. Why do I believe this? The answer is far from fashionable—is, indeed, ancient and passing strange. Fae Malania charged her fierce and lovely words with the drama of one soul's salvation. The stakes were of the highest. In ink she lamented and praised a mortal world that has immortal meaning and where soul matters couldn't matter more. She wrestled with Jacob's bright angel, heedless of the cost, and refused to let go without a blessing.

The Quantity of a Hazelnut

I HAD AN AWFUL dream once, it was a terrible dream, terrible things happened in it. There wasn't any future in my dream. It was all gone, lost, irretrievable; and by my fault, by my own fault.

At the deepest point of my despair, in the twinkling of an eye—though nothing was changed—everything was changed. I was holding—something—in the curve of my palm. Its weight was good to the hand, it was very solid, round. It might have been an apple, or a globe. It was all that mattered, and in it was everything. Even in my sleep, I think I cried for joy.

A long time later, in the *Revelations* of Dame Julian of Norwich, a fourteenth-century English anchoress, I met my dream again, and I knew it at once.

"In this," she says (this vision or, as she always calls it, shewing)—"In this He shewed me a little thing, the quantity of a hazelnut, lying in the palm of my hand, and to my understanding it was as round as any ball. I looked thereupon and thought: 'What may this be?' And I was answered in a general way, thus: 'It is all that is made.' I marvelled how it could last, for methought it might fall suddenly to naught for littleness. And I was answered in my understanding: 'It lasts and ever shall last because God loves it, and so hath all-thing its being through the love of God.'"

4

This is the day which the LORD hath made:
we will rejoice and be glad in it.

I TRY TO MAKE a practice of saying this verse as soon as I wake up, to remind me. Only I have a tendency to answer back. Like "I wouldn't mind rejoicing so much if they'd just let me stay in bed." Or—this morning—"Rejoice and be glad in *this,* what are they talking about?" (Note how the old gods linger, in that "they"— or the Fates or the Furies, or whoever they are.)

It was raining this morning. Well, not just raining. It was trying, with a sort of dull, mindless determination, to blot out the world once and for all. It's still raining. All last night, all day today, where will it end—a steady, meaningless, uninterrupted, unvarying, uninflected *drench,* as if automation had now turned up in nature, to throw individual raindrops out of work.

Rejoice? Oh, I just hate it!

However, let's see now. There's been a drought, and I do care about the food supply, don't I, and the farmers, and the reservoirs? But the farms are mostly in the next county, and the reservoirs are upstate, so why doesn't the rain...? Then can't I summon up a fellow creaturely feeling for the thirsty blades of grass in my own front lawn? Yes, but after all, it rained all night!

I'll never get anywhere like this, trying to aim a theoretical good will at the crops in order to avoid thinking about the rain. What I have to rejoice in—to love and be glad in—is, exactly, the rain. Because the Lord hath made it, and there it is.

O ye Heavens, bless ye the Lord. O ye Waters, O ye Showers, O ye Winds of God, bless ye the Lord. Praise him and magnify him forever. Is *that* what it's doing? Why, yes. I'm the one who's out of tune. My song of praise is full of footnotes claiming exemptions.

This is the world which the Lord hath made, and all his works bless him at every heartbeat of creation, just by being. In the interest of accuracy, I must at least learn to see straight.

When I can see what is really there, as it is in very Truth, as his hands made it and his eyes see it, then—ah, then! Love will come singing, rejoicing, and being glad.

8

UNTIL *LAWRENCE OF ARABIA* I had never actually seen a camel.

Of course I've seen plenty of them processing across Christmas cards, standing around on cigarette packages, sulking in zoos despising their surroundings. The way they look is both laughable and unsympathetic, and suggests that they don't know how to enjoy themselves.

And I've read about them. They are morose, disagreeable, and unloving. They bite their masters. They have neither the generosity to make the best of their lot nor the spirit to put up a really good fight against it. Spiritually speaking, the camel is a total loss.

He is, in fact, a disconcerting reminder of that chilling old theory that God made the world and everything in it for the use of man, and for nothing else whatever. Could God have done such an awful thing? Could he have breathed life into even one creature who is—in himself, for himself—just nothing at all? Created a conscious being to live a life of joyless utility, to be a tool, a convenience, an object? It doesn't bear thinking about.

But now I've really seen a camel.

I've heard one, too—in fact, a whole caravan of them. In the morning when the camp begins to wake, they lift up their voices and greet the day, groaning, bellowing, yawping one after another until the desert roars with a glorious, blaring cacophony. Maybe it's complaint, but there's nothing mean or petty about it. I wouldn't be surprised if that's what brought down the walls of Jericho.

But to really see the camel, you have to see him running. When he walks, lurching and swaying, rolling and pitching, you would think each muscle was headed in a different direction. When he begins to run he's like one of those heavy, ungainly birds who can hardly get off the ground—but when they do, they own the whole wide sky.

Given time enough and desert enough, he manages to get his ramshackle collection of bones all moving together, he picks up speed, stretches out longer and longer, and then... now, there is a *camel!* At full gallop, his neck way out ahead of him, his whole fantastic shape a bewilderment of undulations, fast, powerful, free as a desert storm, he's wild and weird and gorgeous beyond belief, an authentic aboriginal marvel. The whole wide ocean of sand is his; he owns it.

Compared to the camel, the horse is an oversimplification.

Who would ask of such a lord of life that he also cultivate an amiable personality?

I DON'T KNOW MUCH about music, but I know what I like. Why can't I say even that much about people? The attention I pay to the Brahms *Violin Concerto* far surpasses in quality what I give to any human being whomsoever, friend or foe. The concerto is easier, true. But a certain real effort is required, and I do make it— not always, but fairly often.

I settle myself quietly; empty myself of all extraneous thoughts, impressions, emotions; withdraw my attention from all outside sights, sounds, and concepts; and I listen. I turn my whole self to the music like radar; I become a receiver, percipient, minutely alive. I follow in busy quietude the shape of the music as its structure builds in my mind. I say nothing about it to myself, I am for this little space of time a pure act of listening.

I am not simple enough to be very good at this, nor do I have the musical education to hear all there is to be heard. But each time I listen I hear more, and more acutely.

This is surely the clue to the kind of attention I owe to people. I must empty my mind of other claims and, in interior silence, let them tell me who they are. I must remain in watchful, active quiet as the basic architecture of a personality presents itself to my mind. I must learn to hear a slight variation on a theme, a modulation to another key, an inner melody, a discord, an individual beauty of tone.

If love isn't this, it can't be much.

But the minute the note of another human being begins to sound, my self leaps up in clamant alarm and yells: "What about *me?* I'm here *too!*" In the ensuing din, I can't hear a thing.

I have a great deal to learn about the virtue of silence. I wish I could be quiet long enough to figure out how to begin.

PONDERING ON THE nature of contemplation, I have been led to think of my great-grandmother. I don't remember what she looked like, I have never seen a picture of her, I don't remember anyone ever telling me anything about her; and she died, so far as I am concerned, before history began. But I remember her.

I was two (that was the year we went Back Home to visit, so it must have been then). There is nothing at all to say who the woman in my memory picture was—why couldn't she have been just any woman standing in a doorway? But I know.

I was outside the door, on the porch, looking way up at her from my thirty-three inches or so. She was inside, looking down at me, her right hand crossed over in front of her holding the screen door. She couldn't, of course, really have been holding it. In a Southern Illinois summer with a temperature of 108 degrees in the shade and flies and mosquitoes as yet unacquainted with insecticide, nobody held open screen doors. Either I had just gone out and she was closing it, or I wanted to come in and she was opening it. Or maybe she had just given me a cup of cold water from the pump at the kitchen sink. The door was about at midpoint, but I was looking up at her through the screen, not the opening.

It could have lasted no more than a flash of time (otherwise the flies would have got in), but my great-grandmother and I have had all the rest of my life to share this moment, to taste its quality, to assay its meaning. It is still in my mind, perfect, mysterious, unfathomed.

I was looking at her face through the screen, but I don't remember her face. I remember her presence, and a deep, still happiness to be in her presence. I remember the expansion of time, like a slowing of breath, so there was nothing else I had to do but look at her, and grow in the warmth of her sun. There was all the time in the world or there was no time at all any more.

I was trusting and at peace, quite safe. I was entirely myself, simple in substance, of single eye, but peacefully aware of an infinite capacity.

If a moment of true communion with an ordinary, no doubt flawed, human being could be so much to me—a garden enclosed, a stilling of time and temporalities, a flowering of happiness, an intuition of infinite possibility, a secret never forgotten, never fully read.... If all this can be and remain in a moment of human communion, what must it be like to see for an instant the face of God in the shadows, behind the screen? To stand in his presence in still and motionless joy, and know the warmth and shining of his sun?

I keep all these things and ponder them in my heart.

ON MY DINING room table, at the moment, is the magazine section of the *New York Post* from two days ago; half the Long Island paper of the same date; my kitchen timer, put there this morning so I'd know when the eggs were done; my dark glasses; the top of a box I brought home from the bakery yesterday; a pretty little three-minute timer which I used a few minutes ago to take my temperature by (it was normal); today's mail, unopened; this week's *Life;* my checkbook; a checkbook filler; a letter from my mother; a note I wrote to my son three days ago when I left the house; a note he wrote to me the same day when *he* left the house; a cup of coffee, half full; a pencil; a swatch of fabric representing the sofa slipcover before last; the purse I was carrying yesterday, wide open; an empty gray paper bag from a bookstore; a pliofilm wrapper for a pair of white kid gloves which I wore last Thursday; an emery board; two green stamps; a bottle of pills; two foil packets of hand lotion; four flyers from a department store, advertising things I may decide to buy; a pocket edition of the Psalms, KJV; and an album of children's records which I mean to give away, as we're all grown up now.

Also on the same table, the notebook in which I write and my two elbows, supporting the hands that hold my head. What am I to make of all this? (I just took my temperature again and it is still normal; there must be something wrong with that thermometer.)

I know the solution in principle, of course. Pick up any one of these objects, and put it wherever it belongs, and then go on to the next, and so on. On a better day I suppose I could have the table clear in about ninety seconds, or three television commercials. But if this were a better day I wouldn't be telling you all this. Today, I can't. I don't *know* why, that's what I'm trying to explain!

My hand barely begins to reach out toward, for instance, the old newspapers. In a hideous, shivering instant I see everything on the table not as separable, manageable things over which even I might establish dominion, but as a mass, an indivisible glob of things, a surly, lifeless mob of things, a whole more incoherent than the sum of its parts. (God is Three-in-One, but the Devil's name is Legion.)

The brain-to-hand impulse is struck dead, as if by a jealous god.

I turn away and pace (you've seen tigers) to and fro in the house, walking up and down in it. The vacuum cleaner is in the middle of the living room floor. I pause. I could use it or I could put it away; but my mind is not in communication with my hand. I wheel about, my feet take me to the kitchen, where the breakfast dishes are in the sink. I cannot decide to do them, I turn again. The beds are unmade but I swing away, back to the dining room table, to the kitchen, to and fro, up and down. I am very tired, but my unconscious mind is in communication with my legs and I cannot stop. I sit down and then, without knowing how it happens, I am on my feet again, walking.

Do you see? I cannot clear the table, I cannot wash the dishes, which should I do first?

Don't you see, I cannot begin. I cannot *choose* to begin.

Oh, how will I ever explain this to you? Let me try another way.

Over and over I have read and repeated and thought about and clung to and yearned over those words, *All my fresh springs are in thee.* Water, think of it, clear, sparkling, lively, springing up fresh and pure from its source deep in the earth. So all meaningful action springs from a hidden, uncorrupt source.

The mind that chooses, that forms the thought, Let *this* be done *now,* is like the mind that formed the world. Let There Be Light: and Chaos, which was not, began to be filled with all that was. There would be another day for the next step, a separate motion within the mind of God for the moon and the stars, the green herb, the beasts of the field. The mind which decides and orders and instigates has its deep springs in the mind of God.

The hand that reaches out, with knowledge and power, to pick up an old newspaper from a welter of odds and ends is an image of the hand of God. It has authority because it moves, however unknowingly, under the authority of God.

What, then, if the mind cannot choose and the hand is blind, knowing nothing, moving without power or purpose? Chaos is come again.

Chaos is nothing; is Satan. Separate objects on a table are an unintelligible jumble, because the principle of individuation is not in him. The mind cannot differentiate and choose, because in him is no order. The hand can only move blindly in the air, because he does not make, or renew, or restore, or keep, or hold. The feet can only devour the earth, because in him is neither destination nor rest.

From the spring of nothing, nothing will flow.

God, Thou God of the living and not of the dead, send my roots rain.

I SUPPOSE I'D have to say Miss Clements was ugly. It isn't a nice word, and it implies a certain crudeness of perception in the beholder. Fair enough; I was only fourteen, and not uncrude.

In the best of circumstances she could never have been more than plain. But circumstances were not the best. She had a goiter, and one eye drooped; one whole side of her face was indefinably misshapen. She wore a brown silk dress—only one, I *think,* in the three years I knew her—and the hem sagged. Besides, that dress was too long in the first place and anyway it had no shape—ah, here I am, starting an affectionate reminiscence of Miss Clements, and already I'm growing irritable because she didn't fix a hemline.

She used to look at me with love. Christian love. I thought at the time it was just a teacher's pet sort of thing, and made what use of it I could. She was so much under my thumb that I found myself incorporated into the very Body of Christ (she was my Sacred Studies teacher, I forgot to say).

When I decided, or agreed, to be confirmed (and it turned out I had never been baptized, either), I had to think of some respectable reason to give. I had felt religious stirrings, but I didn't regard this as suitable material for conversation. I might have said, "Because everybody's doing it," but that wouldn't have sounded right. What I did say, to others and to myself, was, "Miss Clements asked me to, and I don't want to hurt her feelings."

I think there was more truth in that than I knew. I think I did become a Christian because Miss Clements asked, though not because she asked *me*. It strikes me now that she was on familiar terms with heaven. I see now that she was just the sort of quiet, stubborn type who would pray and pray and never let up, until because of her importunity God arose and gave.

So, without our noticing, incalculable graces come upon us.

Miss Clements died some years ago. She had a Christian name, of course, and I wish I could remember it. I'd like to know her by it now.

I SAW THE MATTERHORN once—just once, for a long moment.

We had come to Zermatt for a day or so, not to ski, just to see the mountain. After the scary cog railway and the walk through the hard and sounding snow we came into our room and I said, "Well, but where is it?"

"Right there," said my husband, pointing out the big window. But there was nothing there, only the snowy hills.

"It's the mist, you can't see it now. But it's there, rising over all the others."

"But there's no mist," I protested, amazed. "It's as clear as can be."

"That's how it looks to you," he answered, giving me a glance of loving concern. "But there is a mist, and the mountain is there."

"It must be awfully far away then."

"Oh no," he said, laughing a little. "Oh no, it's right there."

It is rude to be openly disbelieving of what other people hold to be true, so I said nothing more.

The next morning he was shaking me and laughing and calling, "Hurry up, wake up, it's there, hurry up... ."

I staggered to the window and while I was still saying, "But it *isn't,*" it was. It didn't appear, it *was* there; it had always been there, beyond time, before space, close, alive, huge beyond any scale of comparison. Eternal silence, motionless power, being, perfect act. Presence.

I don't know how long I stood there, rapt, stunned, paralyzed, before that immense and ghostly reality. Then—I suppose the mist came back—I couldn't see it any more. But I knew now.

Sometimes people say, "But how can you really be *sure* God is there?" I can only laugh a little and say, "Oh yes, he's there, he's right there."

I TOOK MY COFFEE out to the porch this morning, putting on my glasses first in case a bird should drop by the birdbath. Instead, a butterfly floated onto the butterfly bush. I have deprived myself of butterflies, I thought sadly. All my life they've been dancing in the air, and I've had my nose stuck in a book. Even now, I'd be reading the *New York Times* except that it didn't come.

Beyond the butterfly bush is a holly tree, higher than the house. Roots, I thought. It has its roots in the earth. The earth holds it stable and straight and strong, the earth feeds it, rain comes to its roots through the earth.

Or is the natural life more like the visible part of the tree? Rooted and grounded secretly, it spreads strong branches on the supporting air, answers sun and rain and wind, embraces in its large courtesy the other lives of birds and butterflies, squirrels and chipmunks and little bright-backed bugs.

Either, or neither, or both. The whole tree lives by the life of God.

And I, planted to grow into a perfect nature, deep and tall and spreading, stunt my branches and wither my roots with malnutrition. In the midst of plenty, I'd rather read a book.

WE SEE THE EMOTIONAL cripple trying to walk, and we shrug and smile at his absurd efforts. We see human beings boxed in, cut off, shouldered aside, the image of God in them dishonored: how good to know it is not our fault! I didn't do it, did you? I am always kind when I can be, aren't you? We see the man caught by sin, and neither cast the first stone nor stay the hand of him who does nor stop to bind the wound. We see the man who makes a nuisance of himself; and after all, it's his own fault that no one listens, that isn't the way to accomplish anything, why is he such a pest? We see the man who is wrong, and since he is wrong he is nothing, of no account, how should we be concerned with such as he?

Our faces turn blank, our eyes glaze, we turn away and go on talking, as if nothing had happened, nothing been said, nothing been seen.

I have been battered and bruised, I am scarred forever by the assault of the blank faces. I have borne (surely in Christ, though for so long I knew it not) as much as I could carry, and more, of this cross. And I bear it still. I cannot lift a telephone and summon up a human voice without fear. I saw the ground open at my feet, I saw the deep abyss. I see it still. Every human contact is to me an act of faith, against my fear, against the pricking of my thumbs.

We are all, all, less than human. I too. I too.

Holy Face of Jesus, teach us what it's like to turn a human face to human pain, and never turn away.

LAST NIGHT I SAW *High Noon* for the first time, on television, and it spoke to my condition. The easy seeping away of support, the withdrawal, the evasion, the turning away, until at last, at high noon, the sheriff is left to face the killers alone on an empty street... and safe inside their houses, the town waits for him to die. All this is what I've been writing about recently, and thinking about forever.

But the movie didn't tell the end.

What happens at one minute past noon, when you've lived that moment and can never not remember? When you've stood alone in the dusty streets, all the doors closed and behind every door someone, a person, knowing you're out there? And afterwards, when the streets are full of people again, pretending to be people again?

What then? Drop your tin star in the dust and walk away? Where to? Another town? Don't you know there is no other town? Here is where you live, or nowhere. This is the town, these are the people, this is the broken, insulted Body. Reparation begins at home.

One minute past noon isn't where the story ends, it's where it begins. The end is love, and the beginning can't begin until love begins.

It happened to me once (to all of us, surely, once?). For reasons further in the past than memory reaches, or deeper in the subconscious than reason reaches, I had always known this moment was on its way. I had seen it come to others—to a person, to a whole people—I had sometimes thought that nearly, it had almost.... But no, it is not so, not yet.

But one day, in the full glare of noon, it was so. The killers were out, and the neighbors closed their doors.

After it was over, there they were again, casually inhabiting the world. What does it matter, they said, everyone always knew they were killers, they aren't worth breaking up our community for, are they? Come back, they said, nothing has happened. Speak to us, they were saying. Look at us. But I couldn't. I can't yet, even behind the safe doors of my heart.

I am still in darkness, before the beginning, waiting for the Light that is to come into the world.

THE ANIMAL KINGDOM holds for us such an infinite variety of delights: beauty, majesty, delicacy, comedy, gaiety, strength, speed, song, grace, grandeur. What a God, to think of such forms to create, such ways of life to set in motion!

But mosquitoes seem unnecessary; buzzards are, to the merely human eye, unattractive; the ferocity of the wolverine lacks the burning-brightness of the tiger. It's the hyena, though, that gives me pause. A more depraved looking animal cannot be imagined. The very sight of him is really nauseating.

But since he is an animal, he cannot be depraved. It is a fault of vision in me that sees that sneaky, ungainly body, those cold intrusive eyes, those hideous, loose jaws, as evil.

God didn't simply install the hyena as you would plumbing, to take care of a sanitation problem. He *made* him. Given what I say I believe of the nature of God, I am absolutely required to believe that he made the hyena with pleasure, looked upon him with love, and saw that he was good. God *enjoys* the *hyena,* just as if he were a meadowlark.

It's thoughts like this that make me realize how little I have yet understood of God.

THIS MORNING IN church, though I was very much present in spirit, I wasn't actually listening at all. Suddenly a bell caught my attention, and words rang in the silence.

For in the night in which he was betrayed he took bread... and gave it... .

My mouth fell open with astonishment and my eyes flooded with tears.

In the dark night of this flawed world where we betray and are betrayed, where it is never safe to put your trust in princes nor in any child of man, this is the great and gracious and healing action we have been given power to do.

In the night in which we are betrayed, we may take the very substance of ourselves and give, to the betrayer, to all them who have forsaken us and fled. With men it is impossible, but with God all things are possible.

I have set my feet on solid rock.

I READ ONCE A very spirited defense of St. Thérèse of Lisieux against the awful charge of being neurotic. What the author was really saying, with considerable heat, was that it was irreverent to suppose that God would perform his mighty works in the souls of inferior people like neurotics. Well.

Let us consider the bare bones of her life: her birth to a mother already fatally ill; the early loss of her mother; the intensity and yet the odd staginess of her relation to her father; that curious childhood breakdown; her lifelong, hungry search for a mother and the shattering loss of one mother figure after another; her "baby of the family" ways and the long agony of self-discipline with which she broke the ties—hands clinging for dear life to the stair rail to keep from throwing away all her gains and flinging herself, again, into the bondage of her human needs.

All this any neurotic can recognize. To say it is normal is to make nonsense of the word "normal" which anyway is nonsense, maybe, but that's not the point. The damage to her personality was done, and cannot be denied. It could not have been her fault. It could never be erased. It did not make her inferior any more than it made her a saint. It was morally neutral, neither good nor bad. It was, simply, what she had been given to live with. *How* she lived with it, and around it and over it and in spite of it and through it, is what made her a saint.

With the same background and emotional equipment she might have become a weepy clinging vine, and everyone would have said, "Oh, Thérèse Martin! She's just a neurotic."

God does not allow defective and damaged minds and hearts to be, and then turn up his nose at them in comfortable superiority, as we do. He gives to *each* human being—and this means the neurotic, the mad, the subnormal— the capacity to be a saint: that is, to fill his vessel full of holiness, here in this life, no matter what sort of odd size or shape that vessel may be.

The saints we know by that name are a very few of the many, each of them a burning and a shining light to illuminate for us some particular facet of holiness. It may be rare for the subnormal to achieve a kind of sanctity from which the rest of us can learn, but I gather that it has been done. The mad are seldom able to live a life that we can make sense of as a model; though, even here, I suspect biographical suppressions or misunderstandings in the lives of a few of the saints. But for the neurotic there is no such difficulty—quite the opposite. If he does become a saint, the flaw in his character will condition his sanctity, shape it, give it its characteristic color and flash; and may make it of particular value to us as a model, since—come now, we're not all that normal, are we?

But whether saints of the church or secret saints or struggling sinners, never mind. Do we really know how many graces come to us from the patient endurance of the mentally deficient who can't even be taught to pray? How much may depend on the bare intent of a soul toward God through one more nightmare hallucination? Can we even guess how the cross is carried behind those terrible and impenetrable veils?

MY HUSBAND LEO says—or St. Benedict says—when evil thoughts come into your heart, dash them against Christ. Leo has been offering me this as a weapon against depression for a long time, but I could never see what it meant. I didn't try to worry it through, because I always do understand Leo in time. But this took longer than usual.

Of course I should have known. I knew the words: *Cast all your cares on him.... Bear ye one another's burdens, and so fulfill the law of Christ.... Surely he hath borne our griefs and carried our sorrows....*

I had even practiced it—in part, obscurely, but with definite intention.

In Charles Williams's novel *Descent into Hell,* the heroine is a girl who cannot even remember a time when she was not afraid. All the sweet custom of dailiness, the simplicity of work and rest and play, companionship and solitude, is alien to her, a foreign country in which others live free citizens, but whose borders she can never cross. She is weighted with pain, crushed and crippled under the yoke of her fear.

Her burden is taken from her by a friend who says, almost this simply, "Here, that's heavy, let me carry it for you." With a definite act of the will, not without cost to himself, he does; and she, lighter by a world-weight, speeds like an arrow home—to the duty prepared for her from before the beginning.

For many months this image swam in my mind like a whale in the deep sea, sounding and surfacing.

Then one day I asked God to let me carry a particular burden for a particular person. I asked every day, day after day, for quite a long while. Then (such are the inscrutable ways of Providence) I completely forgot it, as if it had never happened.

Now—now I remember. And I don't *know*, of course, how could I? But it is true that I have carried a heavy load, these years, and it is true that the person for whom I wanted to carry it has soared like an eagle unchained.

What made me remember was Mary McDermott Shideler's book about Charles Williams—*The Theology of Romantic Love*. She showed me what it was I had been doing, and what it means and how it works, and how much more there is in it than I ever dreamed. Reading that book was like turning on the lights, and seeing shape, color, texture, pattern spring up where before there was nothing but shadowy mass.

Of course I could not lift someone else's pack and carry it myself; neither could Williams's characters. Christ could. And we in him and he in us. No wonder intercession has always seemed so hard. It is really shouldering another's burden, as we may in Christ whose members we are, suffering the pain of the Body, taking—not in metaphor but in plain truth—our real and rightful share in the redemptive work of Christ.

And now I know. So *this* is what I am supposed to be doing! Not presenting God with names of people toward whom I mean well, but performing an *act* of intercession—strict, factual, exact. Not picking up burdens indiscriminately out of pity, either, but just the ones that have my name on them; the ones God has marked for me.

And if I can! If I can learn to do this.... What joy, what unbelievable joy, what a torrent, a flood of joy! To know that in me, in my wobbly, weakling soul, the huge creating energy of the Trinity moves and works.

And even so, I never thought, it never occurred to me, that if Christ bears our griefs—in himself, and through others in himself—then we may simply give them up to him to be absorbed in the marvelous, mysterious health of the Body.

I had—not a grief, but a resentment—an incubus which I could no more cope with than I could move a mountain. So I took it to the altar like a package and, at communion, gave it to Christ. I did not, as Leo and St. Benedict seem to be recommending, throw it at him. I simply handed it to him politely but firmly and walked away without it. And it is true, I am not carrying it now.

Tomorrow I suppose I might snatch it back, all ill-mannerly and grudging, and insist on lugging it about myself. I suppose that *is* possible? I don't know. I don't know anything at all about this way of life, I've only just learned that it is there to learn about. But oh! I feel like Cortes, amazed by the limitless sea.

SO THAT IS ONE way of intercession: substitution of our suffering for others', bearing the burden, feeling the pain. Not just sympathy, and a thousand miles from pity. Coinherence, living within. Filling up in our flesh that which is behind of the afflictions of Christ.

But we are too weak for much of it. Sometimes we can just touch a finger to the cross, sometimes not even that. Even the saints, probably, are shackled to a limited imagination.

That is why the daily office of the church matters so much. This is a prayer we can offer for the merest stranger, for someone we dislike, for a sorrow we haven't encompassed, a problem we haven't understood. We can offer it for a world of hungry children our hearts are too small to hold, for the unknown victim of a sin we've never even thought of, for peace in a world that fills us with a scared surprise.

We can offer it, over and over again, for people we love, and needs we know.

Saying the formal psalms and prayers, following in obedience the rich and ordered prayer of the entire church, adding my small voice to its perfect harmony, I turn the whole river of grace toward those for whom I pray. Not I pray for them. Adam, all Man, prays. The whole church prays. The whole Christ prays.

Let me remember to find a little time for this, even if it means taking a little trouble.

BUT I DON'T KNOW a thing, not a thing, about bearing anyone else's burden.

I walked into a church the other day, brooding darkly over a few wrongs of my own. I thought at first I was alone, but way off in the most inconspicuous corner possible, there was a woman. Crying. Not inconspicuously, either. She tried to quiet down when she heard my steps, but she couldn't.

Oh God, what shall I do, I thought. Shall I be polite and pretend I don't hear her? But she knows I do. Would it be best to go sit down beside her, look her straight in the face, and say, Let me help if I can? Or would that be the last straw?

Oh God, I said accusingly, Why don't you tell me what to do? (And I heard the answer, sadly: You don't listen.)

All right. It is too late to be a saint today, I should have started sooner. But here I am, I have to decide now.

Since nothing in my background or temperament had prepared me to walk up to a perfectly strange woman and ask what she was crying about, I didn't. I closed my eyes and listened. *Do* something! I said fiercely. Help her! Let me!

But she went on crying.

Let me carry it, whatever it is. Let me meet her in the Mystical Body of Christ and, somehow, be of some use. But I didn't know how, and she went on crying.

The weeping never ends, while the world lasts. The blind, the halt, the dumb, the lepers, the beggars, the possessed, and Rachel of the lost children; they go on crying, all of them, and will not be comforted, so long as the world shall last.

If we mean to bear each other's burdens, this is what we must learn to bear: this oceanic tide of weeping, under every song and prayer and praise. It's no good to pick and choose our burdens. We must choose it all, bear it all, and never see the end, never hear the weeping stop.

Bend thy boughs, O Tree of glory. . . .

THERE WERE TWO women living together in one house, and within three days each of them was delivered of a son. Then one of them...but we don't really know what happened.

We see them next in court (1 Kings 3:16–28). One—call her Zillah, I can't keep saying First Woman and Second Woman; but it is a point to be noted that their names are not of record. Zillah, then, has brought an action against Tirzah. She woke in the night, she says, and the child in her arms was dead. But when it grew light, she saw that it was not her child. Tirzah, she charges, has stolen her son, and put in his place her own dead boy.

Tirzah, standing there before the king with the living child in her arms, has only one answer: The child I hold is mine.

King Solomon—lauded to the skies for wisdom, pursued by *sub rosa* murmurings of magic—goes through a flashy bit of abracadabra with a knife, offering to cut the child in half; and "then spake the woman whose the living child was."

But which? Zillah or Tirzah? The king knows, but we do not. That historian, so piously gilding the lily of the king's wisdom, let slip through his fingers the plain story of what happened.

Was it Zillah? Then what Tirzah has done is terrible, but terrible things are sometimes very natural. To reach out for the living child, trying in the moment of death to steal life—who can fail to understand this? It is a disorder native to our flesh. Tirzah, when the first shock of grief is past, will come to her senses.

But if she is the mother of the living child? If it was Zillah who woke and saw her child dead in her arms. She has not reached out for the living, with the living impulse of nature; she has closed her vengeful hands and refused truth. Though one come to her from the dead and say, "Thy child is among us," she will not believe. She will force the king himself to undo the fact and make it happen over again the other way.

Hers is a deeper disorder if that is the way it was.

Or suppose . . . suppose that Zillah, as the light grew, saw the face of the dead child she held, and it was not hers. Suppose, then, that she turned and saw in the arms of the other not a child but a thing that belonged to her. And, in a rage of possession she said, Yes, rather let him be destroyed than that she should have what is mine. The court reporter would certainly have thought, and so recorded, How wise he is, this king. He has found out the true mother. . . . And truly the king was wise, for the child must belong to the mother who gives life and not death.

So many centuries have come and gone since then, so many tongues have told their story, so many living minds have touched their nameless lives, and no one has ever known. History, with its mind on more important things, dumped them out for a useful illustration, and then swept them away under a cloak of silence. All that's left is a cryptic sign, like the crosses along the highway that say: There was a wreck here. But when, of what kind, why, who was hurt and who was left, what real tragedy of real people began here and went on, where and to what end? Silence.

Gentle Mary, Mother of Mercy, lady of silences, rose of memory, rose of forgetfulness, in the deep shadows of thy sheltering mantle hide them, all the silent throng of the world's unrecorded.

IT IS A NATURAL form of prayer for a Catholic Christian to offer whatever comes to hand as a sacrifice for the troubles of his children—a headache, a minor act of self-restraint, a painful illness, a death, even a life. But how much it is against nature to accept the fact that we may profit by their pain.

We are bound to a view of life which is relentlessly sequential. History moves in one direction only, and we feel that our own good is somehow involved in this temporal order. It is right that any man, or a thousand men, should die for the future generation, or for any member of it. But that the child should die for the father is intolerable. It is outrage in the moral order.

Or so we feel. To grasp the nature of our mistake is an intellectual and spiritual upheaval so total you might almost call it a conversion. And still the unreconciled heart continues to twist and turn, denying with its whole animal strength what the mind and spirit say is true.

But there comes a day when you offer not just yourself, but Isaac. Where the flame strikes, there is redemption. There is the cross. Nobody guaranteed there would always be a ram.

But the heart is never reconciled. To the heart, it feels like a long Russian winter, and the baby tossed from the *troika* into the jaws of the following wolf.

No, I can't even apologize for referring to God as a wolf. To use an old and accepted form of words, God is and is not—everything. Including, from this particular *troika,* a wolf.

I don't know what the answer to all this is, but I think I know where it is to be found. When you're hurling yourself, or your only child, out into the howling snow...look straight into the face of the wolf.

IN THE CHURCH of St. Mary the Virgin there is a large and, I used to think, rather ordinary statue of the Virgin. I don't think so any more.

She is simply dressed, in blue I think, with the usual veil. There is a touch of gold in her robe, but I doubt if she has noticed it. Her feet are bare, they stand firm and solid on the ground. Her body is very straight, not rigid but held erect, controlled and unstrained. Her hands are lifted in the position of prayer, but if you look closely you will see that her elbows do not rest against her sides. Though her fingers touch, they are not joined; her hands do not support each other. In spite of the soft, loose folds of her gown, nothing about her is settled or soft or limp. She is all strong bone and disciplined muscle.

Her face is quiet, rather withdrawn, almost a little stern. The marks of suffering are plain, but she is not now suffering, or even thinking about it. She is neither the joyous young mother of the Nativity, nor the *Mater Dolorosa* of the Passion, nor the radiant and serene Queen of Heaven. She is the living, earthly woman who has walked the Way of the Cross with the words still sounding in her ears, *Blessed art thou among women, and blessed is the fruit of thy womb.* She is the mother who has seen the glory of the Resurrected Christ while her arms still ache with the weight of his lifeless body. The whole of her single, sinless soul is concentrated in a single act of containing these impossible opposites, pondering in her heart these fathomless mysteries. Not by the smallest motion of the self does she interrupt the work of God within her.

And yet when you look into her face she does not look away, hoarding to herself a private vision. Her eyes meet yours in pure communication, giving without measure her precious burden of love and fear, of knowledge and of holy hope.

Truly, she is Mary, Mother of contemplation.

IN THE PRAYER for the whole state of Christ's church, I always pray privately for all non-Christian rulers and for the unfaithful departed. But no, not privately, this isn't private prayer. This action of the Mass is the prayer of the whole church, even if only the priest and I are there, and he and I do not agree. He and I are two cells, necessary and small, of one Body. But Christ is *there.* He is who we are, he is who prays.

And if, in me, he prays for the unfaithful, then the Mass is offered for them. He, in his holy wholeness, lifts them up and sees them, offers them, knows them, loves them, makes them whole.

Christ's church is the Mystical Body of Christ. The Mystical Body is the church. Two thousand years aren't enough to know what that means.

We went, recently, to a Salvation Army funeral. Sincerity, devotion, mutual love, a strong, sweet feeling of the presence of the human (yet divine) Jesus. But no outward word of the thick texture of relatedness—membership in an organic, alive One. It was all personal—each person alone with God. Nowhere, ever, have I seen in one place so many beautiful faces, so lit from within.

You can't tell me, I said, that when Mrs. Fair arrived, Christ looked at her and said, "You're welcome, of course, but you were never really part of my Body." Even though they don't seem to know anything about it.... They know a lot about It, my husband said. They know Its ugly sores. They take care of It with their own hands, when nobody else will.

Yes.

But then I always believed the church is all baptized Christians, whether they know it or not. But Pope John, when he saw pictures of Buchenwald, exclaimed "How can this be? The Mystical Body of Christ!"

Yes.

The church is Christ in the world. The cell need not know itself to be.

We, the ones who know, are not the best beloved. We are always with him, and all that he has is ours. The feast is for our brother, who was lost and, in the integrity of the Mass, is found.

"Moreover, O Lord," says St. Ambrose, "I lift up before thee . . . the tribulations of all peoples and the perils of all nations; the sighing of all prisoners and the sorrows of the fatherless; the necessities of them that travel, the wants of the sick, the depression of the weary; the failing powers of all the aged, the aspirations of all young men, the resolutions of all maidens, and the lamentations of all widows."

When the church prays, the whole world breathes. When the Mass is offered, the dismembered world is restored and given back to God. When communion is received, the hungry world is fed.

I WISH I COULD describe the sky of Manitoba. To begin with, it rose from a perfect circle of horizon; even a town in the distance sat flat to the earth beneath it, not reaching into it, not touching it, not altering by a single earthly shape its solid splendor. Clouds and clouds and nothing but clouds, moving fast, standing immense and silent as mountains, brilliant as snow, sun colored, spectrum colored. For days and days they formed and reformed, never a shred of bare blue, clouds beyond clouds beyond clouds in a soundless orchestration of grandeur, glory, abundance. Earth was an insubstantial shadow beneath the vast authority of that Otherness.

One Sunday afternoon, driving across Manitoba under the dominance of the sky, we turned on the radio—a little late—for the news. And heard half a sentence: "...whether the star's death was accident or suicide." We knew at once who it was. Later the announcer said the name, Marilyn Monroe, but we knew already, I think we'd been expecting it.

So God *does* try us above that which we are able to endure? So he *does* send tribulations without sending also the strength to bear them? Oh yes, St. Paul, he does, not everybody has your capacities. Look right here, is not this the victim of a cosmic crooked deck? In what victory will you say this death was swallowed up?

And yet...here is a mystery. God withheld from her the qualities of mind that might have comprehended her terrible life and turned its pain into meaning. But he gave her a spirit so entirely and transparently without malice that she could only be crushed, never twisted, turned away from good, corrupted. So far as is possible to ordinary humanity, she suffered without complicity.

The news finished and, for almost the only time in six thousand miles, the radio abandoned rock 'n' roll and (like a miracle or a message) soared full sail into Scarlatti.

My heart in hiding stirred.

So it ended, not in that sad, small, half-hearted gesture of despair, but in a tranquil and joyous statement of justice in the created order, and—beyond all hope or expectation—the inexhaustible revelation of the sky.

MOST OF US, in spite of pleasant circumstances and fun and games, lead lives of quiet
desperation. Sometimes we hardly even notice
it, supported as we are by a thick web of human
relationships, shored up by a multiplicity of
small pleasures. Other times it's all we can do to
scratch together a few emotional odds and ends
to try to draw a decent veil over the face of reality.

We'd do better to turn and go after it,
instead.

To begin with, never mind pleasure. Search
out joy. Pleasure is its shadow, with no more
substance than a shadow. But joy is real, a secret
splendor running through all creation.

Like gold, it doesn't lie about the streets
waiting to be picked up. It has to be dug for,
with diligence and passion. It's in people, to be
found through the practice of love. It's in work,

in the rigorous exercise of powers of mind or body or spirit. It's a gift the created world is perpetually offering; the price of it is untiring attention to the present moment. It is to be found always and only in the contemplation of reality.

Hunt it down, pursue it, track it to its lair where it dwells. Not in pleasures and pastimes, distractions, piled-up satisfactions, and busyness. It dwells in truth, and nowhere else.

That's why it matters. It will show you moment by moment where truth is for you. And when you know that, cleave to it, turn not aside, be given up to that. That, if you will, is a way of life worth living.

But I haven't really said what I wanted to. There's more than that to joy. Hidden in its glowing heart, light beyond light.... How my blind eyes search the dazzling darkness to find out him whom I have loved, whom I have sought, whom I have always desired.

*All things were made by him, and without him
was not anything made that was made.*

HERE, I THINK, is the heart of the virtue of
poverty. The stripping of the self implies it, of
course, and is needed, but ascesis is never more
than a means. Poverty (a means, too) is nearer
the End—it brings us very near.

The simple, enormous fact that every parti-
cle of matter was called into being—called by
name, itself, alone—through the Word of God
constitutes an absolute demand for the practice
of poverty. If our minds and senses are alive to
the trace of God in all his creatures, we shall
never waste nor spoil nor break. If we take and
eat one piece of bread, how can we drop it half-
eaten and reach for another? If a length of cot-
ton—grown from so miraculous a seed in so
complex a soil, tended and harvested and woven

and shaped by so many hands and minds; product in every atom of God our Father and, through him, of man our brother—if such a scrap of stuff wears thin, shall we not hold it in careful hands? If it tears, shall we not mend it with love?

If we know—with what wonder!—that all things are various, particular, strange, and if we honor in them the work of God who made them, we'll have to use them sparingly. Honoring Bach the maker and Shakespeare the maker, we honor God the Maker, Poet of heaven and earth and of all things visible and invisible. It follows that we won't listen to a fugue and read a sonnet at the same time, disfiguring the image of each with a careless half-attention.

Satiety, haste, boredom, restlessness, indifference, inattention, carelessness—all these are disorders of the soul, and poverty is health. In poverty we hunger and are filled, in the sweet order of God who makes all things new. In poverty we make a deep and joyful reverence to the riches of creation. In poverty we answer with reflected love the potent, generating Love of God.

Because of this, St. Francis sang.

WHEN A GIRL IS accepted to enter the community of our Anglican Poor Clares, she puts on her postulant's dress in the Guest House and then, bare hands and empty pockets, just like that—cold turkey—walks across the lawn to the convent and through the cloister door. No handbag or overnight case; no handkerchief, car keys, library card, aspirin, tranquilizer, Kleenex, comb, toothbrush, driver's license, nail file, postage stamps, pencil, or pen; no bow or brooch, braid or brace, lace, latch, catch, or key to keep back the pure, wild exhilaration of perfect freedom.

But among us ordinary mortals, poverty takes a different turn. I recently began to live a life of relative poverty (well, anyway, low-incomeness) for the love of God and his church. And I was ready for it, glad about it, yes indeed! From now on, I told myself lyrically, accept whatever comes from the hand of God with gratitude. Ask for nothing, refuse nothing. Use it up, wear it out, make it do. Rejoice in the good, simple, plain beauty of bare necessities. Love them. Cherish them. Yes indeed.

But what is this? Brown figured wallpaper where I had thought of cool, white-washed walls? Squares of brown linoleum where I was expecting bare, polished floorboards?

Betrayed into a panic of worldliness, I rush out and buy as much wall-to-wall carpeting as possible to cover as much brown linoleum as possible. Then I settle down to the pious enjoyment of the Holy Poverty of my own choice.

The Christian life is full of these little traps.

THIS MORNING THERE was a pigeon in the middle of East 36th Street who simply would not move, nor even glance up, as our car rolled murderously toward him. Just as I finally screamed, he contemptuously removed himself from under the wheels with the merest flick of a wing. My husband, who had remained calm throughout, remarked: "I can't teach him a thing about New York traffic that he doesn't know already. That's why he's so arrogant."

My husband has a great deal of empathy with animals. Once he told me about an encounter between a June bug and a spider. The drama, the suspense, the universality! Without moving from his chair, Leo flew in the window, all wings and buzz and braggadocio, self-confident and stupid. Then, spiderlike, he marked his prey and placidly elbowed his way toward it, sinister but businesslike. Abruptly becoming himself, Leo scolded the foolish June bug back out the window, then turned on the spider and, in the strongest possible terms, denounced him. The nerve! Sneaking up on defenseless people like that behind their back! In this house the murder of one creature by another will simply not be tolerated!...Nettled, the spider withdrew to his lair to sulk.

"You mean," I said, after I had taken it all in, "you just *left* the spider there? If you wouldn't kill him you could at least have put him outside!"

"But he didn't want to be outside! The June bug came in by mistake, but the spider lives here. When a little fellow creature chooses to make his home with us, we should feel honored, and make him welcome."

"Well, then, if you're going to live with spiders, you have to get used to their killing June bugs. That's the way they are."

"You've missed the point," he said patiently. "Man is supposed to have dominion over all the animals. We're supposed to be in charge. That means if an animal chooses of his own free will to live with us—close to us, within our sphere of influence—he has to conform to our standards. That's the way the world is meant to be."

I wish I'd thought to say, "The spiders, creeping after their prey, do seek their meat from God." But I didn't.

I still occasionally lower the moral tone of the universe by acts of hostility toward small fellow creatures who have sought the protection of our roof. But it troubles me a bit, it really does.

A SPIRITUAL WRITER I've been reading lately informs me that I ought to love God because it is only due to his great goodness that he does not annihilate me right this minute. This gives me a rather vivid insight into the emotions of the downtrodden who are urged to love all their good, kind benefactors. I don't think the comparison is quite so unapt as it may seem, either. I will stick my neck out and say that the question of justice does exist between creator and creature, as well as between man and man.

He also says that, if it is the sacred duty of the child to love its father, how much more are we obliged, etc., etc. Not a word about the duty of the father to love the child.

This is the sort of thing that gives religion a bad name. If we are going to be anthropomorphic (and, as far as I am concerned, we are), why can't we choose the more likable aspects of our human nature to measure God by? Why not assume that he is, at the very least, as good as we would like to be if only we had a little better control over our impulses. We would not, for instance, think about annihilating our child and then decide, graciously and capriciously, not to. We would give him, if we knew how, an oceanic love, joyous, without limit or regret, without afterthoughts or recriminations; and at the same time, a watchful, caring discipline, individually tailored to the child—not to scare him out of his dear little wits but to equip him with a clear-sighted knowledge of the things that belong to his peace, and the moral force and freedom to live by them.

We would not announce that it was his duty to love us. We would say, as a simple matter of fact, that he loves us because we first loved him.

I'm not sure, wicked as I am, that gratitude is the most reliable motive for love. But if God gives us grace to be grateful, let us be grateful not just because he lets us live. So does the government. Let us be grateful for the free, uncost-counting, inalienable, lavish, glorious gift of love.

I DON'T REMEMBER the name of the town, or was it just a checkpoint, where we crossed from Canada into the Montana hills. We were just idling there in the car, thinking of nothing much, while the immigration man brooded over our mixed-up national affiliations. It was hot and bright and quiet, I felt lightheaded from days and days of beauty, my heart was all undefended.

In a split second, without a feather of warning, just the way it always used to happen, the Indians streaked out of nowhere and were upon us. Thundering hooves, lifting cloud of dust, high, bloodcurdling yells, knife-straight black hair swinging, eyes glittering like war fires—they were all around us, ringing us in, cutting off any hope of escape or rescue. There were about thirty of them, mostly about ten years old.

In all my years of Saturday afternoons watching movies in the balcony of the old Uptown, I never saw an Indian charge to match it.

We sat there frozen with incredulous joy while the immigration man laughed at our eastern faces, though kindly. And the tribe swept unchecked across the border, exercising a lost sovereignty with undiminished style, restoring to the wide country its own and ancient name, conferring identity like a blessing by the superb authority of a known and natural presence.

Governments are often useful and often mean well, and must certainly be tolerated. But the land doesn't know them from Adam. So let them remember, from time to time, who's in charge here.

OUR UNCONSCIOUS assumption, I think, is that the love of God most often manifests itself as a sort of pained resignation. And why should it not? He knows us as we are—man, proud man, subject to panic, depression, and rage, slippery as a sneak thief, unlucid and unloving. And yet, we think, he meets our base humanity with a kingly tolerance, a high-minded condescension, a noble refusal to hold a grudge.

This is my commandment, that ye love one another as I have loved you.

And so we do. Little as they deserve it, we are determined to wish them well. We shall not cease to heap on their unworthy heads the coals of our charity; we owe it to ourselves.

Ah, but is this the way God loves? He who laughs and sings with the little hills, who hunts with the lion and exults with the horse in battle, who hides with the wild goat among the rocks when she brings forth her young, is this how he loves? He whose breath is in our nostrils, who sees our bones and has covered us in our mother's womb, he by whose life we live.... Surely in his loving is the whole limitless passion of his illimitable self.

When Israel was a child, then I loved him. I taught Ephraim also how to go, taking them by their arms.... I drew them with bands of love; and I was to them as they that take off the yoke on their jaws, and I laid meat unto them.... How shall I give thee up, Ephraim? How shall I deliver thee, Israel?... Mine heart is turned within me....

O Jerusalem, Jerusalem ....

See how these Christians love one another!

*"Issues from the hand of God, the simple soul." To a
fallen world where no man keeps his brother.**

WHILE HE WAS STILL very young we saw
that he was ill. But there wasn't much we could
do. A few people tried to help, of course, but
they had nothing much to help with, except
bare hands and good intentions. We couldn't
spare much money, though we agreed it was a
shame. We couldn't offer our personal attention,
we were pretty busy.

We knew him in his growing up and in his
young manhood. That is, we saw him around.
We didn't like him much. We could tell he was-
n't getting along too well.

We saw that he always wanted to be on the
other side of every fence, and we took it as a
personal insult. We saw that he was in pain, but
we couldn't help laughing, it was so funny some-

* *The next two reflections refer to the assassination of John F.
Kennedy in 1963.*

times. We saw that he was just barely managing to hang on; and we presented to his unsteady mind a daily spectacle of undisciplined lives, indifferent standards, unreasoning hatreds. Nobody said, remembering his weakness, *I will speak no violence while the world standeth, lest I make my brother to offend.*

We saw that he was alone, and we left him alone.

And one day, to our great moral indignation, he—the one we couldn't find room for in any world of ours—got hold of a gun and started shooting. And the victim was someone we loved and thought we couldn't spare. But weren't they both our brothers? Why were we so willing to spare one of them? Didn't God make them both, not just one of them, in his image?

A man, the day it happened, angrily: "Why are we always so concerned about all these sick types? We're too soft on them!" And a lady, nodding gravely: "We're too lenient. Yes, we are."

The dictionary says that lenient means mild, merciful, gentle, clement . . . *O clemens, O pia, O dulcis!* Were you there when they crucified my Lord?

The earth is soaked with our brothers' blood.
The voice of it cries unto God from the ground
and calls us Cain.

ALL HIS BRIGHT light gone from the world. What can I say, even these many months later, about a death—a life—so numinous? So sun-bright with a truth that darkens the eyes, so formidable with meaning darkly sensed?

What was it we saw in him? Why did we weep so? Why do we still file past that grave in a long, unending line, half in homage, half in a kind of search? What was in him that only our grief told us we had known?

He was the President, and he cared about this country the way we want a President to care; more, he cared about the world the way the world wants a President to care. He thought greatness was possible and was prepared, quite courteously, to insist on it. He thought that meant goodness, too. He was gay and visibly brave, pleasing to look at and fun to listen to. He loved his children, he made us laugh. He died young and, it seemed to us, senselessly. Who could help weeping, all his bright light gone from the world?

But these are details. What we saw in him, behind the accidental splendor of his capacities and accomplishments and personal beguilement, was our own human nature in its splendid, ordinary truth. He swam through flaming seas with a wounded shipmate; but he did it simply, as we might put out a casual hand to save a companion from falling. He made terrifying decisions, for all of us and all the future; but simply and seriously, as we might do our plain best to find the right turn of the road if the wheel were in our hands. Life showered him with gifts and stormed him with blows, opened up to him possibilities and fenced him in with denials, dealt out joy and pain with evenhanded lavishness. And through it all he walked in the glorious liberty of the children of God, enslaved to nothing, refusing nothing, freely choosing to be what he was, to do what was to be done, to bear what was to be borne, fully and strongly engaged in the exercise of all his powers along lines of excellence.

Sun, moon, and stars, being bright, and sent to do their office, are obedient. Man, being bright with a greater light and sent to do a higher office, isn't always. But he was; more than most. In his obedience, he shed about him the true and ordinary human light, the unique image, that is ours alone in all creation, of Light itself; and we were willing for a season to rejoice in his light.

But he was not the first to show us how bright our light might be. There are others, there will be others still, brothers and teachers. Let us begin then, obedient to our office, to study from them how to shine.

IN THE BEGINNING, the disciples came to him and asked, "Where dwellest Thou?" And he answered: "Come and see." Come and see God, come and see Life.

Near the end, when they told him Lazarus was dead, he asked, "Where have ye laid him?" And they answered: "Come and see." Man said to God, Come and see death. Come and see desolation, emptiness, cancellation. Come and see nothing.

Jesus wept.

But he came. He came, like Lazarus, to the grave. Bound hand and foot with graveclothes, a napkin bound about his face, he came to the tomb in the cave with a stone rolled against the door.

One day in Epiphany, reading the words *Behold, the glory of the Lord is risen upon thee,* I had a sudden sharp vision of Christ on the cross—not graciously and symmetrically disposed there as in the usual crucifix, and not in a dramatic agony like a Grünewald. Just dead, plain dead. Battered, torn, bruised, drained, empty, and gone. Dead as a mouse left on the doorstep by the family cat.

From such a nadir the sun of glory rose.

But no, that isn't it. That *was* the glory. Dead or alive, in his birth or in his death, he is all the glory there ever was, or is, or will be, for us. All our emptiness, and desolation, and cancellation, all our nothing, all our thousand deaths of heart and mind and spirit and body, he came to, he saw, he entered into, he took to himself. And behold, they are risen with him.

He descended into our Hell. And now the Light shines in the very deeps of our darkness, and no darkness can ever be deep enough to put it out.

ONE THING THAT cheers me enormously is the barefaced confidence with which St. Peter says, "Lord, thou knowest that I love thee," even though not many days ago he has denied him thrice.

You'd think he might have curled up in a damp ball, moaning, "Oh, I've really ruined everything this time...what will he think of me...it's all very well to say I'll never do it again, but why should he believe that...oh no, I'll never be able to look him in the eye again...."

But not St. Peter. With true apostolic verve, he bounced right back. Bold as brass he made his claim, counting not on his own proven weakness but on the character of his Lord, whom now, at last, he knew.

On those days when everything I touch turns to guilt and gloom and my heart lies limp as a fish within me, I think of St. Peter and mutter stubbornly, "Lord, thou knowest that I love thee."

I'm not so sure, myself, but Lord, thou knowest.

A SAINTLY PRIEST composed a very short morning prayer for busy people, the first third of which is, *O God, I love you.* I could never say that. Spontaneously, of course, if it flew from my heart to my lips without a pause. But not deliberately, with forethought.

What I can say is, *Lord, thou knowest that I love thee.* This phrase, carrying its heavy freight of association, brings the whole church swinging into its wake. It contains within it the defection of St. Peter, the fiery confirmation of Pentecost, the martyrdom of the apostles. It says that my love is firmly grounded in his, fragile and fidgety though it may seem. And other things it says, some that I know now and more that I hope to know hereafter.

But—*O God, I love you.* So flat, so bare, and . . . is it *really* true? It embarrasses me.

The same priest once asked an unbelieving young man to say daily a prayer which began something like this: *O God, if there is a God....* The young man later said that he tried it for a while, but then he began to perceive very faintly the outline of something real behind it; and he didn't like it.

We can't be sure, of course, at this distance, exactly what it was he didn't like. But it does spring to the eye—or ear—that this is no way to talk to God, once you begin to have an uneasy notion that he exists. You don't say "there is a God" in that offhand, inventorying manner, standing in the awesome presence of Him Who Is.

But there *are* words for this: *Lord, I believe; help thou mine unbelief.* If the seeker is unable to say the first phrase, the second alone will do. He may say, *Help thou mine unbelief,* times without number and it may mean nothing to him. But if it begins to show itself a door opening, it will not open directly onto a gangplank. Behind that door is Christ.

Our words, issuing from such a dark and unknown continent within, are full of unsuspected snares, hidden windings to confound the unwary, bottomless pits lightly camouflaged with pretty leafage. They are paths which may at any turn of the way end in a blank wall.

The church's words are paths where we may walk at liberty, in delight and in safety. When we set our feet in them, there is no place to go but to God.

PSYCHIATRISTS, TEACHERS, friends, relatives, and other experts have been accusing me for years of being a perfectionist. I don't mean they are so blind as to think I don't need improving; but my standards, they keep telling me, are absurd. Do I, for heaven's sake, expect myself to be perfect? Who do I think I am, anyway?

At this point the conversation goes to pieces, because we're not talking about the same thing. The theory is clear—I am not perfect, and too much self-reproach over this obvious fact has more to do with pride than with humility. But practice—now that is another matter. At what point may I excuse myself from further effort and say, "I've done all I could, after all I'm not perfect"? This is a practical question and I'd like, if you please, a practical answer.

"I'm so tired I can't do another thing.... I cannot stand this for one more minute.... I have been as patient as anyone possibly could.... I have tried as hard as anybody could be expected to...." None of these statements quite rings true, does it? One more step, ten seconds more of patience, another instant of endurance, another ounce of effort—who can say this is impossible?

Who can say it wouldn't make a difference?

It seems to me, if I'm lying on my deathbed entirely paralyzed except for one finger, and the cat comes up and wants his chin scratched, I'm supposed to scratch it. I don't say I would, or that very many other people would either, but let's not cloud the issue with slighting remarks about perfectionism. The subject of this discussion is charity and grace.

Charity requires me to lift the last movable finger and God will certainly give me the grace to do it, if I ask him nicely. Of course if a friend holds my hand or a scandalized nurse removes the cat, I am thus excused. But I can't just lie there and say I don't feel like it. Who do I think I am, anyway, to deny the universe the full measure of my charity just because I'm dying? (Or exasperated? or in a hurry? or because some scoundrel has treated me less well than I think I deserve?)

Still, we do deny it, you and I and all our friends and relations. Dr. Zhivago said he was dying of lies. I wonder if we're not all languishing away, like genteel Victorian ladies, of anemic imperfectionism.

SOME OF MY BEST friends, like St. Francis de Sales and St. Thérèse of Lisieux, are always going on about the perfection of love and trust to be found in children—the simplicity of the little child who, holding his father's hand, knows he is safe; the effortless goodness of the child who looks to his mother's smile to tell him he is right, and never doubts what he sees in her face.

How can they say such things?

Childhood has always seemed to me a long night of confused shapes and uncertain ground, darkness streaked by nightmare, the devil as a lion seeking whom he may devour, destruction wasting in the noonday. An extreme view, but so is theirs. I think modern psychology leans in my direction.

They talk, these saints, about being with God like a child who, held in his mother's arms, can only babble over and over again, "I love you." But I remember the exact sound of the voice of a little boy, held in an angry mother's arms, who could only babble—howl, rather—"Mother dear, I love you. I *love* you, Mother *dear!*" This incident, seen thirty years ago when I was already not quite a child, has never left my mind.

Still, how can I dismiss all this *gemutlichkeit* as an amiable lack of scientific observation on the part of unworldly priests and nuns? After all, it's gospel. *Except ye become as little children. . . .* He must have meant something.

And I think now I have a clue.

I've been reading about Maria Montessori and what she says are the normal characteristics of the child, the essential personality that is revealed when the conditions of his life are right for him (as in the ordinary course of things they certainly are not).

This "normal" child has an innate love of silence, and a deep delight in attending to the small, living sounds of silence, to the still voice that whispers out of it. He has a love of order and a strong and peaceful will to participate in its creation and preservation. He is open to direction, self-disciplined because he must be to get at the good he sees, cooperative because nothing pinches him. He lives at ease with time, redeeming the moments without haste or anxiety. He has a vigorous and searching intellect which examines, sorts, orders, names, combines, constructs; and is refreshed rather than fatigued by its labors. He works meditatively, seeing the object of his attention with his eyes, handling it with his hands, walking all around it in fact and in spirit, considering it, learning its nature, and from it forming his own. He uses all the materials of his kinetic, sensory, emotional, intellectual, spiritual world in one undivided process of "creating his character." The chief of his ways is joy.

Montessori says there is a "sensitive period" for every phase of learning—what isn't learned at the right time is irrecoverable. At eighteen or so, she says, development stops. After that, the individual just gets older.

Well, maybe. But Jesus does seem to be saying, doesn't he, that we can become as little children?

I mean to find out how.

STANDING AS I DO at the very epicenter of an entrenched and long-established disorder, where shall I put my finger first to say, Let a new life begin? "Don't panic," my husband says. "Remember, God created the whole world in only six days, and he didn't panic."

Mary Ellen Chase says we have lost our sense of enduring values—beauty and quiet, discipline and work. Everyone is always saying things like that, and I always nod solemnly and decide to reform my life. But she said *exactly* that, and so illumined the whole subject that I am really almost persuaded that I will.

It is the order she put them in that is so enlightening. The world is full of women who work far more dutifully and effectively than I do, and if there is a woman less disciplined, I don't see how she gets by at all. Why then are these admirable ladies no closer than I am to "endur-

ing values" (and I don't really think they are)?
Because they've got the order wrong.

Beauty first—and no fly-by-night witchery,
but the kind that can't exist without the rest of
the list. A work of art is created in the quiet of a
mind disciplined, concentrated, drawn in to its
center (even if in no other way is the artist disciplined at all); and with hard labor. The practice of a craft, too, is work, requires discipline
and quiet attention, and results in beauty. A
house cannot be kept in such relative beauty as
is possible for it without quiet, discipline, and
work (if God had set the stars in their courses
and then gone off and left them, the universe
would have been hopelessly snarled five minutes after creation, as every housewife knows).
The work of training a family life into ways (dis-
ciplines) of beauty can be done, if at all, only
with a quiet spirit.

To allow a human soul to develop into anything resembling beauty takes an ocean of interior silence, a large spiritual room to turn around
in. Quiet for thought to form, and moral choice;
for loving contemplation of other people; for
contemplative weighing of how each day is

spent. Quiet of the many voices of the self until the will is, in St. John of the Cross's words, "free, solitary, and pure." How much discipline and work this must take!

But quiet, if it comes first, is a usurper. The perfect silence of the state prison, maintained by excellent discipline and hard work, does not give rise to enduring value.

Discipline, too, can be a lovely thing—the free and rational choice of means in the light of ends clearly known; an intricate simplicity in which nothing is wasted or scattered or scamped. But to what end? Ants are disciplined, but beauty does not result. (Nor, I should imagine, does quiet. Just the tread of all those marching feet must be deafening, to an ant.)

And work alone? Without the shaping of discipline ... without the repose of silence for the soul or the body... neither creating beauty nor keeping it? So must they work in Hell.

Beauty and quiet, discipline and work. For the creation of a world or the conversion of a life, here is a fourfold, single Rule, a little Rule for beginners, containing in it nothing harsh or burdensome to be borne, though a certain strictness may result. And, to further paraphrase St. Benedict, the workshop in which we may diligently practice it is the enclosure of daily circumstance, and stability in all those daily paths which God has prepared for us to walk in.

A SMALL MIRACLE has been taking place right under my nose for years, and I've never even thought about it.

A little plaque of St. Anthony, with the words (in Italian) "Protect our house," has been resting in a rather transient and unregarded way on a ledge in the kitchen for nearly as long as I can remember. An orphanage in Sicily sent it to us in return for a contribution, and since it had already been blessed I couldn't throw it away, so there it stayed, right where it lit.

The miracle is, though everything else in the house collects its weight in dust every day or so, this doesn't. There it stands, pinkly plastic, surrounded by gas fumes, flying grease, and spilling liquids (we are a rather ham-handed family), and for weeks at a time I never go near it. But when it finally occurs to me to wash it, it's as clean as a whistle.

St. Anthony was never a favorite of mine, either. I suppose it's nice of him, in a way, to find things for people; but to tell the truth, it seems a bit trivial. Once in a while, when somebody is really distressed over losing something, all right. But when he constantly allows himself to be so employed, I should think he might spend his whole heaven locating the other glove, and nobody would be a bit the better for it.

Still, how odd, this immunity from household hazard. Can it be a sign, meant for my instruction? Could it be that a saint who appears to me to be wasting his time is in fact doing just what God asks of him?

THERE IS A STORY that Jesus, when he was a child, played at making birds out of clay, and when he tossed them into the air, they flew. Well, I don't believe that. There is another version of his childhood that I believe even less: that sob story about the despised carpenter's family, outcast, poor, hungry, cold, and sad. Nobody despises carpenters nowadays, and I'm sure they didn't then, either, not in that little peasant backwater. There may have been a famine, of course, there so often was; but if everyone else was eating, I think the Holy Family was, too.

I have a different idea of what it must have been like in that holy household. He didn't make birds, but he first, since Adam, named them.

Imagine what it was like watching him grow, seeing his infant eyes first discover a bird and, in delighted recognition, know its nature. What a blazing light of reality must have grown in that house as his world widened, as he saw and touched and handled the common things of the visible world. How the fire must have leapt, how the wood of the table must have shone in the sunlight, how water must have sparkled in the pail, how stone and earth must have described geology. And the flowers beside the door, the wild flowers beyond, the fig tree, the olive, the vine, with what a light they must have burned when the light of his eyes touched them. How the birds must have sung, and the cat purred, and the lambs played. Goats, too, rabbits, butterflies, caterpillars, field mice, little lizards and garden snakes, the ox and the ass, the hen with her chicks, all struck with the lightning of his glance, their natures known and revealed.

How the hearts of Mary and Joseph must have sung, to see the unchanged world in its charged beauty, seeing as he saw.

Those were the hidden years, one with the earth's sweet being in the beginning, Eden in Nazareth. Then he was daily God's delight, rejoicing always before him.

THE ONLY THING you can hope to carry home from a retreat is the habit of recollection, the practice of the presence of God.

The beauty of choir and candles is not exportable, religious emotions don't keep. Devotional practices, no matter how sweet, are ashes in the mouth when they interfere with duty. You may snatch an hour of solitude, but the cat will not observe silence. The meditations and reflections of yesterday, filled with light and joy and strength, were, however, yesterday. Today is today.

In the end the only thing left is God, and God will not be domesticated. You can't build a framework strong enough to hold him.

He is here and now. His voice invites us now, and he is waiting every moment for us to respond.

The trouble is, we're usually back in the middle of last week, poking around under old stones and thinking, where *can* he have gotten to?

IT IS TRUE THAT the voice of God, when we hear it, speaks in the very cadence of our own voice, the very idiom of our own mind. But I don't regard that as cause for suspicion. I can't see why God shouldn't be perfectly at home in the subconscious.

His remarks to me tend to be pretty short and snappy. They usually depress my pretensions, as Jane Austen might have put it; they often make me laugh; and they always—this, really, is why I believe they're authentic messages—they always cheer me up and stiffen my spine. Temporarily, because of my sins, but every little bit helps.

Or sometimes it's a saint conveying the message. For instance: Walking out of my room one difficult, disorganized day, on my way downstairs to a confusion of duties I didn't feel up to coping with, my eye lit on St. Thérèse.

"Help!" I exclaimed, without ceremony. And she: "Go without."

I was really taken aback. And yet it was so like her—so exactly what she would say. I went on downstairs laughing, and got through it all somehow. So, she answered, and refused, and the refusal was all the help I needed. Just the sort of paradox Heaven seems to delight in.

Once, though, God made me a speech so long and so much in my own characteristic vein of sarcasm that I would certainly have doubted it very much if it hadn't been so telling. In church one Sunday morning the priest turned from the altar and said—Christ said, through his priest—"Come unto me all ye that travail and are heavy laden, and I will refresh you."

"Will you indeed!" I murmured, with a sad, sardonic glance up at the crucifix. The answer almost knocked me flat. "What do *you* want with refreshment? I thought you were supposed to be so interested in intercession."

By the time I had recovered from this unsettling encounter we were clear through the consecration and praying that we might worthily receive his most precious Body and Blood, be filled with his grace and heavenly benediction and made one body with him that he might dwell in us, and we in him.

So I went to the altar rail and received, with maybe just a shade less ingratitude than usual, the solid food by which I live. I am nourished, I thought. All that my soul needs to feed muscle and sinew, to build blood and bone, is provided. But the delights of taste, the pleasure of hunger satisfied, the well being of vitality restored— suppose all this is passed along, through me, to someone else?

I have enough. How petty, to begrudge an alms for the poor!

GOD'S IDEA OF what is suitable for us—or even possible—so rarely coincides with ours.

Take Habbakuk. There he was, starting out with a hot dinner for the field hands, when suddenly the Angel of the Lord happened along and told him to carry it to Babylon, where Daniel was in a lion's den. And, I suppose, hungry.

Listen, said Habbakuk, who though a prophet was a reasonable man, I've never even been to Babylon. How on earth am I supposed to find it, let alone find a particular lion's den in it, let alone serve this stew piping hot after I get there?

The Angel, not deigning to reply, just grabbed him by the hair of his head and "through the vehemency of his spirit" set him down in Babylon, in the lion's den. (And Daniel, though pleased, does not appear to have been much surprised.)

Prophet and pottage and lion's den seem a bit remote. But the absurdity of the demand and the vehemency of the spirit—how familiar. The scalp hurts, in memory and anticipation.

THERE IS A rather odd experience I have every once in a while. At night, when I am almost asleep but not quite, I see faces. Hundreds and hundreds of them—or so it seems—in quick succession, caught in a particular expression, laughing, puzzled, angry, troubled, speaking, listening, sorrowing, brooding, just turning away, just now looking up—a million poses, a million faces, never any two alike. So many, I had not thought death had undone so many.

It has occurred to me, belatedly, that these are real faces. Even a great artist can't invent one. He can alter the set of his model's eyes, borrow a bit of his own psychic structure for an expression, add this and subtract that. But to think up a face, starting from scratch, is beyond him. And, of course, beyond me.

So. The faces I see are real. Either people I've actually seen in life, or people who exist (or have existed, or will exist?) and of whom I have some extrasensory knowledge.

In the absence of evidence, let us assume the simpler and more probable hypothesis.

Walking along all the streets of all the cities of my life, all the days of my life, my mind as usual squirreling along in its own tiny absorptions, some faculty in me has been recording with vigilant accuracy every human face my eye has lit upon.

The other day, walking along 42nd Street, I saw the faces that passed for the first time with this same faculty of total vision. They flared in my eyes like lightning, each one a unique culmination of all history, an incalculable dimension of reality, a mystery clothing the miracle of Person. While I was still eclipsed in wonder at one, another came, and another; there was no time to absorb the successive shocks. At the end of a crosstown block I was dizzy with perception, exhausted, almost sick—as I always am from the night visions.

My husband, who has never had the night visions and did not at first understand what I meant about them, has seen the faces in clear daylight for years. But he is not exhausted, he is exhilarated. When he feels depressed he goes out and walks the crowded streets, soaking up faces like a sponge, till the marvel of Adam restores him to joy.

It was only the other day that we began to understand each other, to see that we were both describing the same experience. What still remains to be discovered is why we respond to it so differently.

Perhaps I am not quite ready to share the world with so many sovereign identities, so many new minted images of the King. I'm not quite willing—quite yet—to see them. And so, I am compelled to suffer them.

A PRIEST—NEVER mind who—remarked that his parish was working out very happily. He had just about succeeded, after a couple of years as pastor, in weeding out the undesirables.

Now who do you suppose he meant? Which of the sheep does the shepherd take pains to accidentally lose? Which of its members does he think the Body of Christ would be better off without?

I suppose the low-church dogmatists or the high-church fanatics, depending on his own ecclesiastical persuasion. They must be a real cross, I guess. But ah, let him carry it, and gladly, so that someday all may be one!

Or does he mean the people who always want to run everything? The ones who are always complaining about his choice of hymns? Well, if the church can't put up with them, who will?

Or the women around the place? Another priest prefers to have flowers arranged by the florist because "then you don't have all these women around the place." A man may choose to be a priest, or a lay reader, or an acolyte, or an usher, and so come closer to God's altar. But a woman who yearns after the same closeness is the hereditary foe and must be kept firmly in her place (in the pews, that is, where she may not open her trap except as prescribed by ritual).

Does he mean the lonely ones who have no place else to go and will talk your arm off if you let them? The reminiscent, forgetful, and querulous elderly? What does he want them to do—join a club and stay out of his hair?

Or maybe he means the white racists, the anti-Semites, the haters of this or that. But where are they to go? Who else has the word of life that can give them Life?

Alcoholics? Drug addicts? Perhaps others whose moral strength has been sapped by a physical or psychological affliction? Is Christ's love to come to them only through a friendly bartender or taxi-driver or policeman? If a parish won't tend the wounds of Christ when he suffers in their midst, what on earth is the good of "outreach"?

Can he possibly mean the blind, the deaf, the halt? Those who always have to be led about, explained to twice, waited for, picked up after? Oh no. He has read the Bible, after all. But how about the eccentric, the neurotic, the psychotic, the just plain troublesome? If doctors and social workers and people who sweep the floor in hospitals can throw in a little good will with the daily chores, it seems that a parish would accept with a special joy its quota of oddities. It is a privilege to watch with them in their lonely Gethsemanes. Well worth a bit of boredom and social discomfort.

How reluctant we are (and I don't mean just priests) to give freely what we have freely received, to mediate the love of God to whatever needy and unpromising miscellany God sees fit to send our way. Surely, inasmuch as we have weeded out one of the least of these, we have weeded out Christ.

ONE DAY RECENTLY I found myself puzzled by something that had happened. I wasn't terribly upset or distressed. Just curiously checked. I didn't know what to think, or what to do next.

After the errands were done, I walked—out of my way—to the local Roman Catholic church. I thought I remembered that somewhere in a dark corner there was a St. Thérèse. I found her—a small mosaic high up on the wall right by the sacristy door, with one vigil light burning so I could see her.

And at once, like the click when something falls into place, I knew that I had received a message.

From whom? Thérèse herself would be appalled to have anyone think anything could come from her. She closed her eyes and held out her hand, and whatever God put into it she handed on to others, knowing it was what he meant them to have. I'm sure she does it still.

So, a message from God. Why then this intermediary? I don't know. But I don't have to know. God gives us certain saints as companions of our way, and probably hopes we'll have enough humility and common sense to hold out our hands for what they give us.

The Holy Ghost gave me a push—Go hunt up St. Thérèse and see what she has to say about this. Who am I to stand on my dignity and say I don't need saints? Even so, why did I have to go there? I know little Thérèse very well indeed, I don't need a mosaic to remind me of her. And she certainly doesn't need a mosaic face, or a plaster one, to speak from.

But I walked four or five blocks out of my way on a very cold day (there have been days when I didn't, I wonder how many messages I have missed?) because I felt, vaguely and uncertainly, that there was something there for me. And there was.

It was not a discursive thought with a beginning, a middle, and an end, such as I might have had reading a book or scrubbing a floor. It was a total apperception, present entirely, all at once, to the wordless deeps within me, when I saw her face. Later, I knew it had something to do with humility, and something with simplicity. Later still, a few words began to come, codifying and making available to the conscious mind some part of the, in reality, indivisible material of intuition.

Very little of it is in words yet, or perhaps ever will be. But neither is it gone. In that moment of—I think—direct apprehension of truth (of a small part of truth), truth stored itself in my soul.

But the prosaic drudgery of hauling it up to the surface—translating into clear thought and definite action whatever I can of this given knowledge of humility and simplicity (and of what else?); training my balky, reluctant self to follow as fluently as possible the interior movements of grace—this is of enormous importance, and must not be neglected.

Without this, all might yet be lost.

EVERY RELIGIOUS ORDER, they say (lay order too...why not?), has its own distinctive spirit, its unique style. It sails through the shallows of the world in its own particular way, it launches out into God's deep in its own inimitable way. It is marked, once and for all, by the finger of God, so you can tell it in the dark from any other order in the world.

And at the source of its mysterious, personal life stands the figure, luminous, symbolic, and alive, of its patron saint.

What does this mean, then, for the Order of St. Elisabeth—this little company of women, wives of priests, deacons, and seminarians, who meet on the common ground of trying to shape our lives to our husbands' vocation, to offer our lives as a hidden sharing of their external work? Why has the Holy Ghost given St. Elisabeth to us as a model, and given us to her as raw material to be shaped?

What does God's light look like, when we look at her and see it shining through?

What do we know about her? Well, she was righteous and walked in all the commandments of the Lord—that is, she lived by Rule.

She wasn't anybody in particular, herself— somebody's wife, somebody's mother, somebody's cousin. There were angels all over the place delivering messages, but not to her. It wasn't her prayers that were answered, but someone else's. She wasn't blessed among women, someone else was. It wasn't her child who was the Messiah, it was someone else's. She had a walk-on part.

So happy she was, though, so thankful, to be bearing this ridiculously late, unlooked-for child! I think she must have laughed, like Sarah. It doesn't say so but I can almost see her, bursting into delighted laughter from time to time through the quiet, solitary days, as she hid herself and waited, and kept up with the housework.

And unto her—in such gracious haste!—came Mary, the ark of God, the tabernacle of the Most High, the Christbearer. And—of all things!—saluted her.

Elisabeth, filled with the Holy Ghost, knew that a greater than she was there, and rejoiced. She was the first, not counting angels, to greet the Lady and to stand, and know it, in the presence of the Lord.

Mary remained with her a while, as long as she was needed. Elisabeth was very close to Jesus then, spending her days in a loving companionship of pots and pans and mending and scrubbing, of table and hearth and garden, of feminine chatter and holy silence, of expectancy and joy, with—but of course!—with the church. The Christbearer.

Can we begin to see now, in her, the character the Holy Ghost means to form in us? Obedience, fidelity; a happy and self-forgetful humility; a readiness to be thankful; a quick ear for the voice of the Holy Spirit within us; a discerning eye for the Glory as it is, it really is, in others; a peaceful and loving closeness to Christ, nourished by the simple, daily, household ways of God's household, the church; and always, in all things, generosity, joy.

What barren soil I am for such fruits to grow in! Still, as the angel said, with God nothing shall be impossible.

A CARMELITE NUN sent me, tucked inside her Christmas card, a picture of St. Teresa of Avila. I've put it in my prayer book where I can see it, and have a few words with her, several times a day. It seems to me now that there has always been an empty space there; I just didn't know what was missing.

The most striking characteristic of her face is its expression of absolute realism. In her presence, under that austere and unillusioned gaze, spiritual pretensions die a sudden death.

There are times when I am very much tempted to feel aggrieved about what a saint I might be, really, if only everything wouldn't always be so difficult. One glance at that face and I'm off to the kitchen, reflecting that God is perhaps not greatly moved by the pious sighs of women who haven't done the breakfast dishes.

This, so far as I can gather, is typical of the true contemplative. His eyes are on heaven, but no earthly floor remains unscrubbed.

Since I am called to the scrubbing of floors and the washing of dishes, it is good to be in the company of a saint who insists on plain dealing.

I HATE TO BE out when it's just getting dark. The minute the first lamp goes on, with me on the outside looking in, a polar icecap descends over my soul. I am convinced that I no longer have a home, I'm doomed to wander forever in chill shadows outside the circle of other people's lamplight. (I am an indifferent housekeeper, but a truly devoted homekeeper.)

The other evening after a storm of Christmas shopping, I came slinking home to a dark house at five o'clock on a winter afternoon, my psychic balance out of whack as it always is on these occasions. The house was empty, hollow, unhuman, sullen with silence.

I love silence—I'm always saying so—but sometimes it can be an absence of footsteps, a muteness of voices, a lack of music. I love solitude, but sometimes it can be an absence of faces, a want of living hands and loving eyes.

I switched on all the lights, turned up the furnace, put some Christmas songs (voices) on the gramophone, picked up the cat (purrs), and just sat and shivered, yearning for my two men to walk in the door and make life start again.

"It seemed so cold when I got home this evening," I exclaimed about 11:30 that night. "You've said that five times since dinner," my husband replied kindly. "You've gotten the information across very well indeed. Now what exactly are you trying to convey by it?"

What I'm trying to convey, I suppose, is how good and joyful a thing it is to dwell together in unity. Like precious oil poured out, sluiced out, spilled over, and running in rivers. Like dew falling on the holy hills. God's extravagant blessing and promise of life forevermore.

FROM THE BRIGHT living room—people, books, music, flowers, lamps—I walked up an enclosed staircase into the dark. And with each step my heart breathed peace, opened and flowered into peace.

Surprised, and a little alarmed, I stopped on the last stair and thought about it. I have always hated and feared the dark. Was I now (it was a time of strain and heartache) so tired, so discouraged, so without taste for life that I could walk into a dead blank and feel it a relief?

I stood there weighing my feeling; and no, that wasn't it at all.

It was as if by some psychic accident—*O dichosa ventura*—I had slipped a dimension and walked straight out of all the dailiness of life. Back there in that room were my dear loves and my cares, and a little scattering of all the things

I spend my life with; things I need, things I want, things I would like to be free of.

I went out from them without light, my mind idle, my hands empty—my house at rest. No one watched, not even I. No one saw me. I saw nothing. I walked into the empty dark. And there, where there was nothing in the world of mine, was God.

Safe in the dark, in the lucky night, my heart flowered into peace, flared into love....

NO MATTER HOW shaky the voice in which it is pronounced, a vow seriously taken rings in the clear air of Heaven like the shout of an angel. Rings, and remains.

Kept well, kept badly, kept not at all, it lives in that eternal Now, perfect and unbroken as it was in the beginning. Even the legitimate release from vows that is allowed in this world is, I think, for this world only. The word once uttered in Heaven is truth without condition; and the keeping of it—the living it through to the full term of its being and implication—is the business of eternity.

And did I really say those mighty words, *I will,* on those solemn days? Do those great affirmations still claim me, unchanged and unchangeable by any failure of mine?

Can I, as I promised at baptism, make the awful renunciation, living it through till it rules in all my members, till my frightened, unwilling heart and my wily mind lay down their arms and surrender? Well, by God's help. And because the church has prayed that our Lord Jesus Christ would vouchsafe to receive me and to give me the kingdom of Heaven. And because— later, but in Heaven there is no later—the bishop has prayed that the Holy Ghost may daily increase in me his manifold gifts, and that I may daily increase in him. So it was done, the death by drowning and the new birth. And so, in spite of me, it truly is. To the living of his life I am, in eternity, bound. However long I may delay, he will wait. However meaninglessly I may chatter, my given word still holds.

Another day and another vow, again entering—oh not unadvisedly or lightly—into a new state of being, a holy and honorable estate, adorned and beautified with Christ's presence. Wilt thou love him, comfort him, honor and keep him. . . ? *I will.* And have I always. . . ? Do I ever? *I will.* This union, too, is fact in the sight of God: one flesh saying with one voice, *I will*, until each separate self yields up its last stony patch of self and is lost and given back again—

oh stunning courtesy!—in that one which once was two. If not here, then There, no matter. The vow stands until it is totally fulfilled.

Still another day, another vow, but this one not mine. The day when Leo entered without me into another new state of being: when he was called, with awesome simplicity, to feed and provide for the Lord's family.* That great *I will* is his and only his. But since other spoken words have made us one, he could not speak this word without my assent. As he shares in the one true priesthood of our Lord, may I not share with Mary the joy of being unnecessary, and yet uttering to the listening Heaven a necessary assent? (Oh, I speak as a fool! But what else can we do, constrained by vows to follow majesty at whatever limping distance we can?)

Others still, not mine.... One day, a new profession of faith in baptism. Another day, another kind of profession—to me a mystery—in a monastery choir. From these, too, I am not shut out; in these I have a share through the grace of our Lord Jesus Christ and the love of God, and in the communion of the Holy Ghost. I hear the voices sound in Heaven, echoed by the quite

---

* *Leo Malania was ordained to the priesthood in the Episcopal Church in 1964.*

unnecessary, so blessedly permitted, assent of my love.

And in perfect correspondence to every voice and every vow, what bright realities of being! What a glory of transfigurations, all that is truly human remade and blazing in the light of God.

HOW I AM STRAITENED, with all these many deaths to die! The first, when I was baptized into Christ's death and born again of water and the Spirit, I accomplished as easily as an infant, and with no more idea than an infant of what I was about. The last, the death of the soul to God, from which there is no resurrection, I hope (being an heir, through hope, of an everlasting kingdom) that I may escape.

The death of the body, that heavenly birthday from which we wake to life eternal, I suppose I shall get through like everybody else, one way or another. (St. Thérèse, who took so long to die, in such pain, said, "I no longer believe in myself dying. . . . I shall never be able to manage it. . . .")

But oh, *this* death, the death of self, so that I may truly say I live—yet not I, but Christ lives in me. How many death struggles and I survive!

No, I cannot believe in myself dying this death. . . . I shall never be able to manage it.

Except a corn of wheat fall into the ground and die, it abideth alone; but if it die, it bringeth forth much fruit.

I should be glad of another birth.

PERMISSIONS

THIS BOOK, practically every page of it, is alive
with quotations from the Bible and the liturgy; and
there are lines, and echoes, and variations from other
writers, too. The quotation on page 4 is from *A
Shewing of God's Love,* by Julian of Norwich,
superbly edited and partially modernized by Sister
Anna Maria Reynolds, C.P. (Longmans, Green and
Co., London, 1958).

On page 49 the words in the last paragraph, "lady
of silences, rose of memory, rose of forgetfulness,"
are from T. S. Eliot's "Ash Wednesday." The first line
of page 75 is from "Animula"; though Eliot puts it in
quotation marks and doesn't say where he got it. I
believe, but am not sure, that it is Duns Scotus. "So
many, I had not thought death had undone so many,"
on page 109, is from "The Waste Land," and Eliot
himself took it from Dante. The last line of "Journey

of the Magi" and the last line of this book bear a remarkable resemblance, and also a difference—I remembered Eliot, but meant something else. All these poems are from *Collected Poems, 1909–1962* (Harcourt, Brace).

Gerard Manley Hopkins is another whose words appear often in my thoughts, and so appear here. The last line of page 19 is from "Thou art indeed just..." "My heart in hiding stirred," on page 58, is from "The Windhover"; "no bow or brooch," and the rest of that long line from "The Leaden Echo and the Golden Echo" will be found very slightly altered on page 64. "The earth's sweet being in the beginning," on page 101, is from "Spring." All these, from *The Poems of Gerard Manley Hopkins* (Oxford University Press).

Shakespeare is here too, and Keats, Blake, Thoreau, and Henry Vaughan; and a sprinkling of saints: John of the Cross, Benedict of Nursia, Thérèse of Lisieux. If a thing is worth saying, somebody has usually already said it, often too well to tamper with. My respectful thanks to them all.